BOOK OWNER DETA

Thank you so much for your purchase, If you like this book I would greatly appreciate a review. (this will really help my book stand out among the thousands).

If you are interested in receiving free printable versions of this book and many others, simply scan the QR code below with your phones camera.

This will bring you to my facebook page, where you can receive your free download.

WHETHER YOU ARE A FIRST TIME BUYER OR AN EXPERT AT RENOVATIONS, IT IS EXTREMELY HELPFUL TO RECORD EVERY DETAIL, THIS PLANNER WAS DESIGNED TO MAKE YOUR RENOVATION MUCH EASIER.

FROM COSTS, QUOTES, PURCHASES, WARRANTY & GUARANTEE DETAILS, INTERIOR DESIGN IDEAS, LAYOUTS.

THIS HANDY HELPER INCLUDES:

Interior Design
Make note of the room dimensions, plan which colors, furniture, lighting, accessories, flooring and much more.

Layout / Floor Plan
Dotted grid page, so you can sketch out how you would like the room to be laid out.

Task To Do List
Checklist for you to record tasks/jobs for that room, eg; Call plumber to install kitchen tap.

Quotes Page
Record your quotes for that room, which company, Job/task description, cost, and your thoughts on them, eg; too expensive

Purchased Furniture & Items
Control your budget, track your purchases for each room, add them up to give you a total cost.

Renovation Material List
Track building material costs & important information.

Notes
A page for notes for each room - Record Ideas, appointments, alterations, problems, soloutions, etc.

Stress Relieving Colouring Pages
Whether you want to release some tension or are simply waiting around for plasterer to turn up, these colouring pages will help.

ORDER OF CONTENTS

HOUSEHOLD BILLS

COST PER MONTH

BILL	PROVIDER	YEAR 1	YEAR 2	YEAR 3

MAJOR APPLIANCES

APPLIANCE	
BRAND	
SUPPLIED BY	
DATE PURCHASED	
COST	
MODEL / SERIAL	
WARRANTY	
DIMENSIONS	

APPLIANCE	
BRAND	
SUPPLIED BY	
DATE PURCHASED	
COST	
MODEL / SERIAL	
WARRANTY	
DIMENSIONS	

MAJOR APPLIANCES

APPLIANCE	
BRAND	
SUPPLIED BY	
DATE PURCHASED	
COST	
MODEL / SERIAL	
WARRANTY	
DIMENSIONS	

APPLIANCE	
BRAND	
SUPPLIED BY	
DATE PURCHASED	
COST	
MODEL / SERIAL	
WARRANTY	
DIMENSIONS	

MAJOR APPLIANCES

APPLIANCE	
BRAND	
SUPPLIED BY	
DATE PURCHASED	
COST	
MODEL / SERIAL	
WARRANTY	
DIMENSIONS	

APPLIANCE	
BRAND	
SUPPLIED BY	
DATE PURCHASED	
COST	
MODEL / SERIAL	
WARRANTY	
DIMENSIONS	

KITCHEN - INTERIOR DESIGN

ROOM DIMENSIONS ______________________

OF WINDOWS ____________ # OF DOORS ____________

WINDOW 1 SIZE ____________ DOOR 1 ____________

WINDOW 2 SIZE ____________ DOOR 2 ____________

WINDOW 3 SIZE ____________ DOOR 3 ____________

COLOR / STYLE ______________________

WALLS ______________________

FLOOR ______________________

CEILING ______________________

TRIM ______________________

DOORS ______________________

NOTES / IDEAS

KITCHEN LAYOUT PLAN

KITCHEN - TO DO LIST

TASKS	DONE

KITCHEN - QUOTES

DATE	COMPANY	SERVICE/JOB	PRICE	THOUGHTS

KITCHEN - FURNITURE & ITEMS

DATE	ITEM	SUPPLIER	COST
		TOTAL	

KITCHEN - MATERIALS LIST

DATE	ITEM	SUPPLIER	COST
		TOTAL	

NOTES

STRESS RELIEF / BOREDOM

LIVING ROOM - INTERIOR DESIGN

ROOM DIMENSIONS ______________________

OF WINDOWS ______________ # OF DOORS ______________

WINDOW 1 SIZE ______________ DOOR 1 ______________

WINDOW 2 SIZE ______________ DOOR 2 ______________

WINDOW 3 SIZE ______________ DOOR 3 ______________

COLOR / STYLE ______________________

WALLS ______________________

FLOOR ______________________

CEILING ______________________

TRIM ______________________

DOORS ______________________

NOTES / IDEAS

LIVING ROOM LAYOUT PLAN

LIVING ROOM - TO DO LIST

TASKS	DONE

LIVING ROOM - QUOTES

DATE	COMPANY	SERVICE/JOB	PRICE	THOUGHTS

LIVING ROOM - FURNITURE & ITEMS

DATE	ITEM	SUPPLIER	COST
		TOTAL	

LIVING ROOM - MATERIALS LIST

DATE	ITEM	SUPPLIER	COST
		TOTAL	

NOTES

STRESS RELIEF / BOREDOM

DINING ROOM - INTERIOR DESIGN

ROOM DIMENSIONS ______________________________

OF WINDOWS ______________ # OF DOORS ______________

WINDOW 1 SIZE ______________ DOOR 1 ______________

WINDOW 2 SIZE ______________ DOOR 2 ______________

WINDOW 3 SIZE ______________ DOOR 3 ______________

COLOR / STYLE ______________________________

WALLS ______________________________

FLOOR ______________________________

CEILING ______________________________

TRIM ______________________________

DOORS ______________________________

NOTES / IDEAS

DINING ROOM LAYOUT PLAN

DINING ROOM - TO DO LIST

TASKS	DONE

DINING ROOM - QUOTES

DATE	COMPANY	SERVICE/JOB	PRICE	THOUGHTS

DINING ROOM - FURNITURE & ITEMS

DATE	ITEM	SUPPLIER	COST
		TOTAL	

DINING ROOM - MATERIALS LIST

DATE	ITEM	SUPPLIER	COST
		TOTAL	

NOTES

STRESS RELIEF / BOREDOM

MASTER BEDROOM - INTERIOR DESIGN

ROOM DIMENSIONS ____________________

OF WINDOWS ____________ # OF DOORS ____________

WINDOW 1 SIZE ____________ DOOR 1 ____________

WINDOW 2 SIZE ____________ DOOR 2 ____________

WINDOW 3 SIZE ____________ DOOR 3 ____________

COLOR / STYLE ____________________

WALLS ____________________

FLOOR ____________________

CEILING ____________________

TRIM ____________________

DOORS ____________________

NOTES / IDEAS

MASTER BEDROOM LAYOUT PLAN

MASTER BEDROOM - TO DO LIST

TASKS	DONE

MASTER BEDROOM - QUOTES

DATE	COMPANY	SERVICE/JOB	PRICE	THOUGHTS

MASTER BEDROOM - FURNITURE & ITEMS

DATE	ITEM	SUPPLIER	COST
		TOTAL	

MASTER BEDROOM - MATERIALS LIST

DATE	ITEM	SUPPLIER	COST
		TOTAL	

NOTES

STRESS RELIEF / BOREDOM

BEDROOM 2 - INTERIOR DESIGN

ROOM DIMENSIONS ______________________

OF WINDOWS ____________ # OF DOORS ____________

WINDOW 1 SIZE ____________ DOOR 1 ____________

WINDOW 2 SIZE ____________ DOOR 2 ____________

WINDOW 3 SIZE ____________ DOOR 3 ____________

COLOR / STYLE ______________________

WALLS ______________________

FLOOR ______________________

CEILING ______________________

TRIM ______________________

DOORS ______________________

NOTES / IDEAS

BEDROOM 2 LAYOUT PLAN

BEDROOM 2 - TO DO LIST

TASKS	DONE

BEDROOM 2 - QUOTES

DATE	COMPANY	SERVICE/JOB	PRICE	THOUGHTS

BEDROOM 2 - FURNITURE & ITEMS

DATE	ITEM	SUPPLIER	COST
		TOTAL	

BEDROOM 2 - MATERIALS LIST

DATE	ITEM	SUPPLIER	COST
		TOTAL	

NOTES

STRESS RELIEF / BOREDOM

BEDROOM 3 - INTERIOR DESIGN

ROOM DIMENSIONS ______________________

OF WINDOWS ____________ # OF DOORS ____________

WINDOW 1 SIZE ____________ DOOR 1 ____________

WINDOW 2 SIZE ____________ DOOR 2 ____________

WINDOW 3 SIZE ____________ DOOR 3 ____________

COLOR / STYLE ______________________

WALLS ______________________

FLOOR ______________________

CEILING ______________________

TRIM ______________________

DOORS ______________________

NOTES / IDEAS

BEDROOM 3 LAYOUT PLAN

BEDROOM 3 - TO DO LIST

TASKS	DONE

BEDROOM 3 - QUOTES

DATE	COMPANY	SERVICE/JOB	PRICE	THOUGHTS

BEDROOM 3 - FURNITURE & ITEMS

DATE	ITEM	SUPPLIER	COST
		TOTAL	

BEDROOM 3 - MATERIALS LIST

DATE	ITEM	SUPPLIER	COST
		TOTAL	

NOTES

STRESS RELIEF / BOREDOM

BEDROOM 4 - INTERIOR DESIGN

ROOM DIMENSIONS ______________________________

OF WINDOWS ______________ # OF DOORS ______________

WINDOW 1 SIZE ______________ DOOR 1 ______________

WINDOW 2 SIZE ______________ DOOR 2 ______________

WINDOW 3 SIZE ______________ DOOR 3 ______________

COLOR / STYLE ______________________________

WALLS ______________________________

FLOOR ______________________________

CEILING ______________________________

TRIM ______________________________

DOORS ______________________________

NOTES / IDEAS

BEDROOM 4 LAYOUT PLAN

BEDROOM 4 - TO DO LIST

TASKS	DONE

BEDROOM 4 - QUOTES

DATE	COMPANY	SERVICE/JOB	PRICE	THOUGHTS

BEDROOM 4 - FURNITURE & ITEMS

DATE	ITEM	SUPPLIER	COST
		TOTAL	

BEDROOM 4 - MATERIALS LIST

DATE	ITEM	SUPPLIER	COST
		TOTAL	

NOTES

STRESS RELIEF / BOREDOM

BEDROOM 5 - INTERIOR DESIGN

ROOM DIMENSIONS ______________________

OF WINDOWS ______________ # OF DOORS ______________

WINDOW 1 SIZE ______________ DOOR 1 ______________

WINDOW 2 SIZE ______________ DOOR 2 ______________

WINDOW 3 SIZE ______________ DOOR 3 ______________

COLOR / STYLE ______________________

WALLS ______________________

FLOOR ______________________

CEILING ______________________

TRIM ______________________

DOORS ______________________

NOTES / IDEAS

BEDROOM 5 LAYOUT PLAN

BEDROOM 5 - TO DO LIST

TASKS	DONE

BEDROOM 5 - QUOTES

DATE	COMPANY	SERVICE/JOB	PRICE	THOUGHTS

BEDROOM 5 - FURNITURE & ITEMS

DATE	ITEM	SUPPLIER	COST
		TOTAL	

BEDROOM 5 - MATERIALS LIST

DATE	ITEM	SUPPLIER	COST
		TOTAL	

NOTES

STRESS RELIEF / BOREDOM

BATHROOM 1 - INTERIOR DESIGN

ROOM DIMENSIONS ______________________

OF WINDOWS ____________ # OF DOORS ____________

WINDOW 1 SIZE ____________ DOOR 1 ____________

WINDOW 2 SIZE ____________ DOOR 2 ____________

WINDOW 3 SIZE ____________ DOOR 3 ____________

COLOR / STYLE ______________________

WALLS ______________________

FLOOR ______________________

CEILING ______________________

TRIM ______________________

DOORS ______________________

NOTES / IDEAS

BATHROOM 1 LAYOUT PLAN

BATHROOM 1 - TO DO LIST

TASKS	DONE

BATHROOM 1 - QUOTES

DATE	COMPANY	SERVICE/JOB	PRICE	THOUGHTS

BATHROOM 1 - FURNITURE & ITEMS

DATE	ITEM	SUPPLIER	COST
		TOTAL	

BATHROOM 1 - MATERIALS LIST

DATE	ITEM	SUPPLIER	COST
		TOTAL	

NOTES

STRESS RELIEF / BOREDOM

BATHROOM 2 - INTERIOR DESIGN

ROOM DIMENSIONS ______________________________

OF WINDOWS ______________ # OF DOORS ______________

WINDOW 1 SIZE ______________ DOOR 1 ______________

WINDOW 2 SIZE ______________ DOOR 2 ______________

WINDOW 3 SIZE ______________ DOOR 3 ______________

COLOR / STYLE ______________________________

WALLS ______________________________

FLOOR ______________________________

CEILING ______________________________

TRIM ______________________________

DOORS ______________________________

NOTES / IDEAS

BATHROOM 2 - LAYOUT PLAN

BATHROOM 2 - TO DO LIST

TASKS	DONE

BATHROOM 2 - QUOTES

DATE	COMPANY	SERVICE/JOB	PRICE	THOUGHTS

BATHROOM 2 - FURNITURE & ITEMS

DATE	ITEM	SUPPLIER	COST
		TOTAL	

BATHROOM 2 - MATERIALS LIST

DATE	ITEM	SUPPLIER	COST
		TOTAL	

NOTES

STRESS RELIEF / BOREDOM

BATHROOM 3 - INTERIOR DESIGN

ROOM DIMENSIONS ______________________________

OF WINDOWS ______________ # OF DOORS ______________

WINDOW 1 SIZE ______________ DOOR 1 ______________

WINDOW 2 SIZE ______________ DOOR 2 ______________

WINDOW 3 SIZE ______________ DOOR 3 ______________

COLOR / STYLE ______________________________

WALLS ______________________________

FLOOR ______________________________

CEILING ______________________________

TRIM ______________________________

DOORS ______________________________

NOTES / IDEAS

BATHROOM 3 LAYOUT PLAN

BATHROOM 3 - TO DO LIST

TASKS	DONE

BATHROOM 3 - QUOTES

DATE	COMPANY	SERVICE/JOB	PRICE	THOUGHTS

BATHROOM 3 - FURNITURE & ITEMS

DATE	ITEM	SUPPLIER	COST
		TOTAL	

BATHROOM 3 - MATERIALS LIST

DATE	ITEM	SUPPLIER	COST
		TOTAL	

NOTES

STRESS RELIEF / BOREDOM

ENTRANCE/HALLWAY - INTERIOR DESIGN

ROOM DIMENSIONS ______________________

OF WINDOWS ____________ # OF DOORS ____________

WINDOW 1 SIZE ____________ DOOR 1 ____________

WINDOW 2 SIZE ____________ DOOR 2 ____________

WINDOW 3 SIZE ____________ DOOR 3 ____________

COLOR / STYLE ______________________

WALLS ______________________

FLOOR ______________________

CEILING ______________________

TRIM ______________________

DOORS ______________________

NOTES / IDEAS

ENTRANCE/HALLWAY LAYOUT PLAN

ENTRANCE/HALLWAY - TO DO LIST

TASKS	DONE

ENTRANCE/HALLWAY - QUOTES

DATE	COMPANY	SERVICE/JOB	PRICE	THOUGHTS

ENTRANCE/HALLWAY - FURNITURE & ITEMS

DATE	ITEM	SUPPLIER	COST
		TOTAL	

ENTRANCE/HALLWAY - MATERIALS LIST

DATE	ITEM	SUPPLIER	COST
		TOTAL	

NOTES

STRESS RELIEF / BOREDOM

GARDEN - DESIGN

MEASUREMENTS

COLOUR / STYLE

FENCE

GROUND

LIGHTING

SEATING

DECKING

<u>NOTES / IDEAS</u>

GARDEN LAYOUT PLAN

GARDEN - TO DO LIST

TASKS	DONE

GARDEN - QUOTES

DATE	COMPANY	SERVICE/JOB	PRICE	THOUGHTS

GARDEN - FURNITURE & ITEMS

DATE	ITEM	SUPPLIER	COST
		TOTAL	

GARDEN - MATERIALS LIST

DATE	ITEM	SUPPLIER	COST
		TOTAL	

NOTES

STRESS RELIEF / BOREDOM

________________ - INTERIOR DESIGN

ROOM DIMENSIONS ____________________

OF WINDOWS ____________ # OF DOORS ____________

WINDOW 1 SIZE ____________ DOOR 1 ____________

WINDOW 2 SIZE ____________ DOOR 2 ____________

WINDOW 3 SIZE ____________ DOOR 3 ____________

COLOR / STYLE ____________________

WALLS ____________________

FLOOR ____________________

CEILING ____________________

TRIM ____________________

DOORS ____________________

NOTES / IDEAS

__________________ LAYOUT PLAN

________________ - TO DO LIST

TASKS	DONE

_______________ - QUOTES

DATE	COMPANY	SERVICE/JOB	PRICE	THOUGHTS

________________ - FURNITURE & ITEMS

DATE	ITEM	SUPPLIER	COST
		TOTAL	

________________ - MATERIALS LIST

DATE	ITEM	SUPPLIER	COST
		TOTAL	

NOTES

________________ - INTERIOR DESIGN

ROOM DIMENSIONS ____________________

OF WINDOWS __________ # OF DOORS __________

WINDOW 1 SIZE __________ DOOR 1 __________

WINDOW 2 SIZE __________ DOOR 2 __________

WINDOW 3 SIZE __________ DOOR 3 __________

COLOR / STYLE ____________________

WALLS ____________________

FLOOR ____________________

CEILING ____________________

TRIM ____________________

DOORS ____________________

NOTES / IDEAS

______________________ LAYOUT PLAN

______________________ - TO DO LIST

TASKS	DONE

________________ - QUOTES

DATE	COMPANY	SERVICE/JOB	PRICE	THOUGHTS

____________________ - FURNITURE & ITEMS

DATE	ITEM	SUPPLIER	COST
		TOTAL	

________________ - MATERIALS LIST

DATE	ITEM	SUPPLIER	COST
		TOTAL	

NOTES

Printed in Great Britain
by Amazon

63829328R00072